CHRISTMAS COVENTRY
AT FOOL HOLLOW

POETRY
IN SOLITUDE

CHRISTMAS
COVENTRY
AT FOOL HOLLOW

S.C. WATSON

Christmas Coventry at Fool Hollow: Poetry in Solitude

For information about this title or to order other books and/or electronic media, contact the publisher:

Baja Bad Press, LLC
bajabadpress@gmail.com

ISBNs:
978-1-7346376-3-2 (hardcover)
978-1-7346376-4-9 (softcover)
978-1-7346376-5-6 (eBook)

Printed in the United States of America

Cover and Interior design: 1106 Design
Cover Art and Illustrations: Andréa Watson

For all who seek truth

CONTENTS

Preface	xi
The Fisher King's Dream	5
La Nochebuena	9
Birth, Our Birth	15
Hear Him	18
Christmas Prayer	23
The Plague (Rome, Italy, 1630)	28
Snow Falls Blue	32
Apache Teardrops	36
November	40
Desert Daughter	43

Tombstone Winds   46

Cassie's Cabin   49

Superstition Sunrise   53

The Ghost Stallion of Superstition Mountain   57

Lazuli   63

Mexico   67

Soledad   69

The Wasp   71

My Heart Bleeds Azul   73

Baja Bad   75

Surfin' Scorpion Bay   78

La Dama of the Sea   81

The Wharf   83

From my Cabin on Fool Hollow Lake   85

Ana's Love   87

Alejandra   89

Ozzy   91

Time   92

Psychedelic Lies   94

Laura's Lair   96

The Mōg   100

La Tirana   102

Baja Black   104

Apparition 31   106

La Sirena   109

Holy of Holies, Mountain Fire   114

The Olive Press   118

Omphalós   123

The Nazca Lines   126

Liahona: Light of Paracas?   127

About the Author   133

PREFACE

The written word is the single most effective means of communicating thought over time and space; indeed, it is our portal for literary participation in the great conversation of humankind. Writing appeared suddenly on the historical landscape of our various cultures and civilizations, as if by divine design, rather than intellectual evolution, and despite natural entropy. In its purest expressions, it is art. Perhaps the loveliest form of language arts is poetry. Its traditionally concise and carefully crafted sounds, rhythms, imagery, symbolism, and technical devices echo the senses, inspire the imagination, and enlighten both our personal perceptions and collective understanding of the universe.

Poetry is beauty, and beauty is truth, absolute truth. And we seek after it.

Some of the poems in this collection are lyric, structured with stanzas, rhyming lines, and meter, generally iambic tetrameter; others are haiku and conventional chiasmi. The haiku contain seventeen syllables in three lines of five, seven, and five, centered on natural imagery. Haiku traditionally focus on one moment in time and are meant to be read aloud in a single breath. A few of the haiku include a string of interwoven haiku, while others incorporate chiastic elements and structure, an original form the author calls "haiX," or chiastic haiku.

All of the poems are intended to evoke thoughts of the Divine, and his love for humanity and creation. In many instances, the themes include death, addiction, isolation, and winter. While these subjects may seem inherently dark, the author attempts to address them in a life-affirming manner.

The term "Coventry" originally stems from the Saxon village of Coventry, birthplace of St. George, dragon slayer and patron saint of England. A few of the poems allude to dragons, camels, hawks, magi, and royalty, conveying actual and legendary images from both medieval and early Christian eras. In addition, the term "sent to Coventry" refers to the deliberate ostracism and isolation of another. Certainly, the years 2020 and 2021 were periods of relative voluntary and involuntary Coventry.

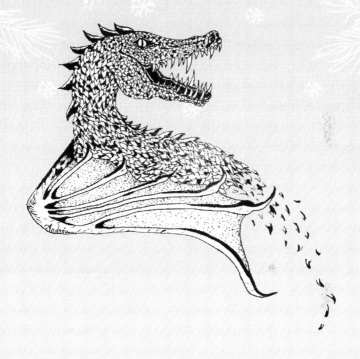

The Star became the Light.

The Lamb became the Shepherd.

And the Shepherd is the Light of the World.

Snow-dusted lone pines

Bristle in the dry, white wind:

Cold, dead, hollow men

Pale conspiracy,

Moonlit ravens' cobalt glow:

Artificial snow

The Fisher King's Dream

"Whom does the Grail serve?"

Wounded Fisher King,
Guardian of the Goblet,
Fishes a dead stream
And dreams: rock gardens,
Cherry blossoms in spring's breeze,
Clear, cool mountain pools.

Soldiers take the field;
Archers line stone castle walls.
Burst bright, black powder!
Self-inflicted wound
Bleeds blue; equinoctial stars
Shroud sepulchral clouds.

Burnt oaken timbers'
Ash snows bury gold embers:
Famine's dry wasteland.
England's tattered flags
Hang like pale, wind-blown corpses;
David's sword shattered.

Perceval arrives,
Adorned in silver, bestride
Arthur's white stallion.
Impaled Fisher King,
Guardian of the Hallows,
Wakes, and glances up.

His skeleton realm
Desolate, dun, war-ravaged;
And he, without heir.
Brave knight dismounts, kneels,
Bows his head in sworn respect.
Easter's moon rises,

As the gallant chevalier prays:

"Wounded Fisher King,
Guardian of Christ's Chalice,
Whom does the Grail serve?"

Snowflake-glazed aspens

Below a Mōgollon moon

Stream silver starlight

Ethereal light

Penetrates coal firmament;

Reveals bright new orb

LA NOCHEBUENA

She crossed the border on Christmas Eve
Eight years old with bandaged knees
She read the Bible beneath the stars
Hoot owls tolled the passing hours
She prayed that God would grant her power
Mustangs knelt in desert flowers
She prayed that God would grant her power
Mustangs knelt in desert flowers

She crossed the border on Christmas Eve
Little girl about to freeze
Shivering child on a winter night
Dreamed 'til the stars slipped from sight
She woke with the silver morning light
Took mother's hand and held it tight
She woke with the silver morning light
Took mother's hand and held it tight

La Nochebuena, Christmas Eve
Saguaro cactus, mesquite trees
La Nochebuena, Christ is born
Sonoran sunrise, desert morn'

She crossed the border on Christmas Eve
Ducked barbed wire, black swarming bees
Hid in a cave from a passing plane
Knelt in cactus, winced in pain
Scorpions scurried between her feet
Stale tortillas and beans to eat
Scorpions scurried between her feet
Stale tortillas and beans to eat

She crossed the border on Christmas Eve
Wiped her face on dirty sleeves
Torn cotton blouse, worn Wrangler jeans
Rusty water, dry canteens
Walked lonely miles under cloudless skies
Tears fell from swollen, tired eyes
Walked lonely miles under cloudless skies
Tears fell from swollen, tired eyes

La Nochebuena, hail the King
Coyotes trumpet, creations sing
La Nochebuena, hail the King
Coyotes trumpet, creations sing

She crossed the border on Christmas Eve
Eight years old with bandaged knees
Imagined shepherds on grassy knolls
Camels packing silk and gold
A brilliant star over Bethlehem
A baby, Jesus, King of Men
A brilliant star over Bethlehem
A baby, Jesus, King of Men

She crossed the border on Christmas Eve
Little girl, but she believed
Removed a cross from around her neck
Wrapped it in a handkerchief
Climbed to the top of a jagged rock
Left her gift and humbly walked
Climbed to the top of a jagged rock
Left her gift and humbly walked

La Nochebuena, Christmas Eve
Saguaro cactus, mesquite trees
La Nochebuena, Christ is born
Sonoran sunrise, desert morn'

She crossed the border on Christmas Eve
A red-tailed hawk caught the breeze
Circled low above her frail frame
Eastern wind whispered her name
"Maria, Maria, do not fear,

Sweet little child, I am here
Maria, Maria, do not fear,
Sweet little child, I am here"

She crossed the border on Christmas Eve
Eight years old, finally free
Daughter of God, sun, and sand
Alien child in an alien land
Maria died that Christmas night
Walks with angels on trails of light
Maria died that Christmas night
Walks with angels on trails of light

La Nochebuena, hail the King
Coyotes trumpet, creations sing
La Nochebuena, hail the King
Coyotes trumpet, creations sing

Singular blue spruce

Stands true against the ice wind;

Bids Christmas begin

Rabbit tracks across

White powder, disappear like

Indian summer

Birth, Our Birth

In a simple stable
   Behind a crowded inn
She humbly bore our Lord,
   King of women and men

The Savior of mankind,
   He humbly bore our sins
Near the brook of Cedron
   In an olive garden

Humbled magi kneel

Before the child, King of Kings;

Heavenly choirs sing

Suffer the children

To go unto Him; behold,

The children suffer

Hear Him

Hear Him knock, lost souls—
  Earth's deep valleys shall be filled,
Her mountains made low.

Immersed in water,
  All righteousness, He fulfilled;
Straightway He rose, Lord:

Jesus Christ

White dove descended;
    Spirit, upon Him lighted.
The Father praised Him.

Witness of the Light,
    All flesh shall see salvation—
Hear Him, world; He knocks.

19

Dragon's breath ices

Purple in the punishing

Wind beneath stone wings

Three holy Dragons,

Saddled in purple and gold,

Ascend their light thrones

Snowflakes from heaven

Waltz in the solstice moonlight:

Fairy princesses

CHRISTMAS PRAYER

(traditionally sung in a round)

Stockings hung in a neat little row
Her fire burns with a warm winter glow
Christmas tree trimmed with tinsel and lights
She longs to hear the children laugh tonight

Gaslights burn on each dark city block
Their candles lit, they dance as they walk
Carolers dressed in mittens and scarves
They sing beneath the moonbeams and the stars

Church bells ring out that Christmas is here
Our faith burns bright; we pray peace is near
Believers bow to Father above
We hope to know His everlasting love

Slate-blue kestrels dance

And dive under pogonip,

Like autumnal leaves

Rooftop sentinels,

Piercing icicle daggers—

Hang, midnight watchmen!

Darkness falls, moonrise;

Santa boards his magic sleigh.

"Wake, 'tis Christmas day!"

I don't trust anyone who doesn't play chess, and I certainly don't trust anyone who does. But my computer has no genuine personality or sense of humor, and I desperately crave human interaction.

THE PLAGUE

(Rome, Italy, 1630)

She floats down cobbled Spanish stairs
Dances as they sleep
Candles consume the direful air
Rome kneels at her feet

Conquers heroes, now marble-winged
On chariots of gold
Dreadful winter witch, she brings
Cruel death and cruelest cold

Dark angel from a distant land
Dry whirlwind in the leaves
Vision of horror, sword in hand
Life shivers in her breeze

Drifts across still, ancient gardens
Pauses where grapes are crushed
Dips her toes in holy fountains
Kisses yon master's brush

Wanders Michelangelo's halls
God's creation o'er her head
Haunts long-hallowed Vatican walls
Paints paths of sick and dead

Demon born of eastern lands
Harsh tempest on the seas
Pandemic blown by wind and sand
Rome's faceless, evil queen

Pandemic zombies,

Faces shrouded in silence,

Shuffling about town

Living as you choose

When so many around you

Die as others choose

Snow Falls Blue

Snow falls blue
On the mountains tonight
Deep and dense in the aspen groves
Your angry words
Consume my mind
Like mesquite in my potbelly stove

I'm crazy cold
On the cabin floor
Sippin' my last shot of Patrón
Wind whistles hard
Through my old oak door
Down through my chimney of stone

Snow falls blue on Flagstaff
The powder masks my pain
Crazy cold in Flagstaff
Ice runs through my veins
Wind whistles hard through Flagstaff
Tequila clouds my brain

You left me here
To wither and die
Like the leaves on the silver trees
You and this bottle of venomous lies
Shook my soul
And burned my dreams

Snow falls blue on Flagstaff
The powder masks my pain
Crazy cold in Flagstaff
Ice runs through my veins
Wind whistles hard through Flagstaff
Your memories remain

Cabin solitaire—

Applewood fire glows garnet;

Wolves howl in my woods

Deep in my mind's caves,

Dire wolves shadow my spirit—

Fire through nightmare eyes

Apache Teardrops

Apache teardrops from the sky
Mustang warriors, painted colts
Leap of honor, a choice to die
Thunder clouds, lightning bolts
Apache teardrops from the sky
Mustang warriors, painted colts
Their women watch, and softly cry
A thousand tears, and wonder why

Apache teardrops in the cold
Snowflakes frozen in the rocks
Blood and blankets bought and sold
Treasures each teardrop unlocks
Apache teardrops in the cold
Snowflakes frozen in the rocks
Sacrificed for land and gold
Legends passed on by their old

Apache teardrops fall like rain
Ghost tears of obsidian
A witness to the white man's reign
Symbols of a senseless sin
Apache teardrops fall like rain
Ghost tears of obsidian
Pursuit of never-ending gain
Great Father, when will evil end?

Burrowing owls breathe

Hollow's damp alfalfa must;

Sup on bunkhouse mice

Desperate hopes dwell

Adown Fool Hollow's waters,

Abiding judgment

November

On that first November
With its first blue snow
We fell in love together
Believing love would grow

On that first November
With its first blue snow
What was meant forever
Was nothing we will know

We were sure of ourselves
So in love with each other
If only you could see
You're a part of me
The other side of me
It's not living without your love

On that first November
With its first blue snow
Words were lost on letters
And dreams I'll never know

I was sure of myself
So in love with you lady
If only you could see
You're a part of me
The other side of me
It's not living without your love

Darkling mallard drake,

Solo on Fool Hollow Lake:

Christmas Coventry

DESERT DAUGHTER

Last winter she lost her way
Packed her pickup and left AJ
Desert daughter from a redneck town
Like a lightning storm before sundown
Singing to a country beat
Guitar lying across her seat
Black cowboy boots, apache wild
Half desert angel, all native child

Desert angel, stay with me
Desert angel, I'll set you free
Desert daughter, feel the sun
Play your music; love's just begun

Last summer she found her way
Packed her pickup and left LA
Desert daughter in an asphalt town

Like a flower buried under ground
She traveled ten thousand miles
Played her music, true to her style
Captured the soul of her native land
Spoke to their hearts like rain to sand

Desert angel, trust in me
Desert angel, I'll set you free
Desert daughter, feel the sun
Play your music; life's just begun

Skipping flat, round stones

Across placid mountain lakes:

Summer ambition

TOMBSTONE WINDS

Blood and whiskey mark the sands
Outside saloons like cattle brands
Summer storms wash outlaws' plots
Tombstone winds sweep desert lands

Whores and horses bought and sold
Like apple pies with miners' gold
Winter snows melt into streams
Tombstone winds blow bitter cold

Tombstone winds across the land
Time and sand erase the pain
Tombstone winds echo the men
Tombstone rains erode their claims

Rope and hangmen signal death
Desperados gasp for breath
Easter flowers breathe new life
Tombstone winds aren't all that's left

Tombstone winds across the land
Time and sand erase the pain
Tombstone winds echo the men
Tombstone rains erode their claims

Sage saguaro tribes,

Arms raised to turquoise heavens:

Prayerful desert pleas

CASSIE'S CABIN

She weathered winter winds
Where snow falls fast on plains
Was once a mountain inn
With stained-glass windowpanes

She housed Wells Fargo riders
Who rode the Great Divide
With bags of silver dollars
And gold from the Blackhawk Mine

Prairie dogs bark at passing stars
Whistling through the ice-gray sky
Miners drink in woodland bars
Where hoot owls and banshees cry

A blue moon rises above the plains
Like a lantern in the dark
A blue moon rises above the plains
Like smoke from a steam train's stack

She's splintered cedar, termite dust
Hand-molded red clay bricks
Iron pipes buried deep in rust
Covered in weeds and sticks

Yet Cassie's cabin remains
Though a ghostly memory now
Of mining towns and midnight trains
One dreamer's last sundown

Red rocks brace for snowfall
On a chilly Denver eve
The north wind rumbles through the hills
Past cottonwoods and evergreens

A blue moon rises above the plains
Like a lantern in the dark
A blue moon rises above the plains
Like smoke from a steam train's stack

Indigenous deer,

Precious reservation does—

Run hard. Run free. Run.

Life's merciless rest—

Wild mustangs on dry meadows:

Hungry, homeless vets

Superstition Sunrise

Superstition sunrise
Streams sunlight through pale blue eyes
Indian cycle between your thighs
Superstition sunrise
A dry wind blows from the West
Crystal locket swings against your breasts

Superstition sunrise
Your sunlight blinds my eyes
Superstition sunset
Your sunset shades my cries
Superstition sunrise, ride desert lows
Superstition sunrise, breathe desert highs

Superstition sunrise
Leather jacket, silver ties
Heartache ringing in your hollow lies
Superstition sunrise
I sense doubt within your soul
A dark roadblock takes truth's painful toll

Superstition sunrise
Your sunlight blinds my eyes
Superstition sunset
Your sunset shades my cries
Superstition sunrise, ride desert highs
Superstition sunrise, breathe desert lows

Superstition sunset
Fading taillights turn to gold
And girl, this poor biker's gettin' old
Superstition sunset
Your sunset shades my road-tired eyes
And I know too well love always dies

Superstition sunrise, live desert highs
Superstition sunset, die desert lies

Canyon echoes death,

Claws etched in black patina:

Sacred grizzly glyphs

Ravens hold vigil

As corpse-green fog settles low,

Thick on frosty ponds

The Ghost Stallion of Superstition Mountain

Beyond red hawk mountain shadows
Purple portals encased in stone
The mustang stallion Thunder
And a hundred ghost mares roam

Monsoons flash like silver
Rains pummel the midnight cold
Over rocks and rotting timbers
Run the legends, fierce and bold

White Bison King and Gila Prince
Summon demon hordes from hell
Their warriors battle to the death
Bound fast by evil spells

The Dutchman's curse is a whisper
Scrawled in blood and cherry wine
Thunder rushes like a windstorm
Through the beams of the old man's mine

A poison arrow fells Cochise
He slips from his charcoal steed
Coyotes howl in cruelest glee
With fury and frenzy feed

Flames engulf the catacombs
Smoke fills the cavern caves
Villages burn like wooden tombs
Torched by angry braves

Princess Dreamsong hails the harvest moon
And a thousand trailing stars
She prays Thunder returns soon
To deliver them from war

The Dutchman's curse is a whisper
Scrawled in blood and cherry wine
Thunder rushes like a windstorm
Through the nightmares of her mind

They splash across gold dust streams
Trample yellow cactus flowers

Past lonely lakes where bullfrogs sing
Late in the evening hours

A covey of quivering quail
Hide beneath a mesquite tree
Hooves beat-black the desert trail
Bones rattle in the breeze

The herd ascends the mountain halls
Pierces the veil of fears
Crashes through the granite walls
Hidden where no man dares

The Dutchman's curse is a whisper
Scrawled in blood and cherry wine
The Dutchman's curse is a whisper
From a world that turns back time

Beyond red hawk mountain shadows
Purple portals encased in stone
The mustang stallion Thunder
And a hundred ghost mares roam

Monsoons flash like silver
Rains pummel the midnight cold
Over rocks and rotting timbers
Run the legends, fierce and bold

Blood flows fast like the lava falls
At the heart of Earth's crimson core
Thunder screams out the battle call
As they charge through crumbling doors

The Dutchman's curse is a whisper
Scrawled in blood and cherry wine
Thunder rushes like a windstorm
Through the beams of the Dutchman's mine

Blue apparition,

Winged, gossamer phantasma:

Fallon's flighty sprite

Discarded shoes hang

From an ancient cottonwood

Like abandoned lives

LAZULI

(as in the blue gem, lapis lazuli)

Lazuli, remember me
Guitar in a country bar
Lone Star lady, set me free
Waltz across my whiskey floor
Lazuli, remember me
Waltz across my whiskey floor

Lazuli, dance for me
Merlot lips and sapphire eyes
Apache angel of my dreams
Wrap me in your Wrangler thighs
Lazuli, dance for me
Wrap me in your Wrangler thighs

Lazuli, remember me
Love me all eternity
Lazuli, set me free
Bathe me in your sapphire eyes
Lazuli, set me free
Love me all eternity

Lazuli, return to me
Mountain moonlight, silver stars
Desert demon, set me free
Midnight marks the witchin' hour
Lazuli, return to me
Midnight marks the witchin' hour

Lazuli, remember me
Love me all eternity
Lazuli, set me free
Bathe me in your sapphire eyes
Lazuli, return to me
Love me all eternity

Tarantula hordes

Migrate north through Texas towns

Whispering, "Freedom"

Across the river

People dream and children die;

Do walls absolve us?

Mexico

Night crawls across crimson sands
Death howls at the moon
Blood runs between desert lands
Soldiers coming soon

Stars shoot across open skies
Sun rises and sets
They sell us their tortuous lies
From corporate jets

A wind blows from Mexico
The dust blinds my eyes
A wind blows from Mexico
I hear their cries

Drugs and guns, and hungry souls
Bought and sold each day

When will this dark hatred end?
Hear. And act. Then pray.

A wind blows from Mexico
The dust blinds our eyes
A wind blows from Mexico
We hear their cries

SOLEDAD

Her prison's a bottle of Cuervo Gold
And a trailer in Abilene
She drinks and sleeps in the desert cold
Crossed the border at seventeen

The money she makes she sends her son
Who lives in a boarded-up store
A lonely skeleton lost on the run
Been told his mother's a whore

Soledad's a sinless soul in the wind
Crossed the border at seventeen
She crossed the border at seventeen
Crossed the border at seventeen

She dreams of a Juarez boy and talks
Of margaritas in the sun

But now her flesh and spirit she hocks
At the end of a sheriff's gun

Soledad's a sinless soul in the wind
Crossed the border at seventeen
She crossed the border at seventeen
Crossed the border at seventeen

A silver cross around her neck
A rosary in her hands
Beautiful child in a desolate land
Lost on the desert sands

She crossed the border at seventeen
Crossed the border at seventeen
Soledad's a sinless soul in the wind
Crossed the border at seventeen

THE WASP

Sun-scorched lips on a dry canteen
A pack full of tortillas and weed
His bloody wounds blister gangrene
As he bakes on a rock and bleeds

A bullet tears through his Levi jeans
Barbed wire slashes his back
He's running on fear and refried beans
And, the sting,
He longs for death

The wasp descends with lightning speed
Glitters gold with wings of steel
The hornet preys on all it sees
Glitters gold, and poor men kneel

The wasp strikes hard
Round after round
He stumbles in the cactus and sand
The migrant buckles as he hits the ground
White bandana flag in his hand

The wasp descends with lightning speed
Glitters gold with wings of steel
The hornet preys on all it sees
Glitters gold, and good men kneel

MY HEART
BLEEDS AZUL

My heart bleeds azul
My days without you
My heart bleeds for you
If only you knew

If only the lies you whispered were true
If only the days I spent were with you

My dreams are azul
My nights without you
My dreams are of you
If only you knew

If only the visions I dreamed were true
If only the nights I spent were with you

My heart bleeds azul
My life without you
You say that we're through
My heart bleeds azul

If only the lies you whispered were true
If only the visions I dreamed in blue
If only the life I shared were with you

My heart bleeds azul
My heart bleeds azul

Baja Bad

Got habaneras on the grill
Rattlers in the fryin' pan
My Stratocaster pays the bills
I'm playin' in a Baja band
Maria's dancin' gives 'em chills
Playin' in a Baja band
I'm Baja bad, I'm Baja bad
Playin' in a Baja band

Cold Coronas buried in ice
Cheap Havanas, Bandit can
Texas hold 'em, every vice
I'm playin' in a Baja band
Mezcal sunset paradise
Playin' in a Baja band
I'm Baja bad, I'm Baja bad
Playin' in a Baja band

Tequila everywhere I go
Rock and roll renews my soul
I'm Baja bad, but all alone
Baja bad in Mexico

Livin' out of beachfront bars
Wrangler's parked in the garage
Four-twenty underneath the stars
I'm playin' in a Baja band
Maria's dancin' gives 'em chills
Playin' in a Baja band
I'm Baja bad, I'm Baja bad
Playin' in a Baja band

Tequila everywhere I go
Rock and roll renews my soul
I'm Baja bad, but all alone
Baja bad in Mexico

Red tide foam sparkles,

Hallucinogenic waves;

Surfers' blood moon fades

Surfin' Scorpion Bay

Time stands still on Scorpion Bay
Like seashells in the sand
The steel-gray surf is weapons-grade
Reminds me of Thailand
Beach camp bonfires, Modelos
Cantina's closed again
I grab a wad of worn pesos
And eat at Alacran's

Baja pizza, adobe ovens
Mesquite burns in the air
Sweet Andrea's touch, like heaven
Red rose in her Aztec hair
Inked skull and cross-boards above her ass
Bikini and high heels
Don Julio from a pink shot glass
Shuffles the cards and deals

Scored weapons-grade on Scorpion Bay
Scored killer waves all day
Time stands still on Scorpion Bay
Scored killer waves all day

Like shack-time in a hollow wave
Time freezes in the bar
She's everything you'd ever crave
I wager my sports car
Time stands still on Scorpion Bay
Like slivers in the sand
Pack my guitar and walk away
My car keys in her hands

Scored weapons-grade on Scorpion Bay
Scored killer waves all day
Time stands still on Scorpion Bay
Scored killer waves all day

Midday sun glistens

Through a million particles,

Christening the waves

La Dama
of the Sea

Seal suit and seaweed hair
On a waxed, white board, she rides
Sun-kissed skin in the salty air
La dama smoothly glides

Shoots the curl of a six-foot wave
Like a princess of the sea
A dolphin pod sails and dives
Her companions swift and free

The waves roll endless, warm, and blue
Scatter driftwood on the beach
The waves paint stories in the sand
Broken shells beneath her feet

The orange sun sets slowly
At her kingdom's western wall
And the *pueblo*, San Clemente
Sleeps 'til the seagulls call

The waves roll endless, crimson red
Driftwood bonfires on the beach
The waves paint stories in the sand
Broken shells beneath her feet

THE WHARF

The dark scent of smoked fish
Meanders up through
Adobe shafts and stone chimneys
Up damp corridors
Where blue moss clings
To rusted iron gratings—

I load the cargo deck and curse
The smell of salt and tuna blood
And tired, dingy, rotting berths

And curse the heavy seabirds' calls
And silent schooners now beyond
The purple stone marina walls

And curse the lonely chill of dawn
The azure fog across the bay
And then move on—

The dark scent of smoked fish
Streams high into the lazy night
A dim light from the boathouse
Warns of jagged rocks ahead

Up into the cadaver-blue fog
Wanders the gray stream,
Vanishing

From my Cabin on Fool Hollow Lake

His breath, fast and warm
Her neck like porcelain
Young angels, island-born
Mere shadows in the wind
Ivory dress, sheer and torn
On mossy granite stones
Long blond tresses, gently blown
About his signal horn

Impassioned lovers, aroused
Tangled in the weeds
Isolated from town
Beneath palo verde trees
Suddenly, all senses stoked
A cloud of lively bees

Sheltered only by her skirt
From chilly autumn breeze

Storm whips hard, September gale
Sweeps red Caribbean seas
Lovers run, hand in hand
Down rocky cactus trail
She falters once, and glances back
On romantic schoolgirl dreams
Eyes locked, souls life-sworn
Though path autumnal black

Sailor's moon glows pale blue
Waves pound the pirate shore
Tempest billows skeleton-palms
And docks where vessels moor
Love dances in the gathering squall
A thousand seagulls soar
Storm-pillaged, but hearts true
And sure, forevermore

Ana's Love

Once in a lifetime you meet the one
Who steals your heart away
Then disappears like Sonoran sun
Over Rosarito Bay
You sense his soul in the ocean mist
He speaks to you in the wind
You remember that night you last kissed
And you long for him again

Ana's love's a catamaran
Tossed and tilted by the sea
Ana's love spans ocean and sand
The soulmate of her dreams

He comes and goes like the breaking waves
Whispers her name in the shells
Like a seagull's call on a cloudy day

His voice echoes in the swells
He's a silver moon in swaying palms
Reflected on silken sands
And he's always her one true love
Though a sand castle in her hands

Ana's love's a catamaran
Tossed and tilted by the sea
Ana's love spans ocean and sand
As she dreams of what will be

He forever steals her heart away
As her sunsets turn to years
He slips beyond the bounds of day
Only daybreak dries her tears
He's rock music at the festival
He's the sea breeze on her face
He's the hues of a Sonoran rainbow
And he's everything she tastes

Ana's love's a catamaran
Sails a vast eternal sea
Ana's love's a song and a man
Who waits for when she's free

ALEJANDRA

Alejandra sips red sangria
Salsas in the summer rain
Dreams of a boy in Barcelona
Lights a cigar and breathes his name

Alejandra dances with a stranger
He holds her close in hands of ice
Steps through puddles of smoke and anger
Sleeps in a wine-laced paradise

Alejandra sips red sangria
Longs for the love she left in Spain
Alejandra dreams of Barcelona
Dwells in a world of pleasure and pain

Alejandra lives in San Diego
Money and a mansion, exotic cars

Drinks and stares out bayfront windows
At silent yachts and distant stars

Alejandra sips red sangria
Longs for the love she left in Spain
Dreams of a boy in Barcelona
Dwells in a world of pleasure and pain

Ozzy

(with a nod to Percy Bysshe Shelley)

I met a Mayan made of clay
Sun-baked skull on Scorpion Bay
Piranha eyes, a jaguar smile
I guess he'd tarried quite a while
"Look on my works," he once declared
But in those days no one had dared
"Hail Ozymandias!" they cheered
"Hail great King Ozymandias!"

But where's thy scepter? Where's thy throne?
Where's thy temple? Where's thy great hall?
Where stands thy legion? Now just bones?
Where's thy treasure? What of thy soul?
Oh, Ozzy, Ozymandias
Forgotten Ozymandias

TIME

Time streams through narrow glass
Sands dance as hours pass
All time ends in sorrow
All time is but borrowed

Time fills my hourglass
Time waits beyond my grasp
Time slips into the past
Time slips into the past

Time drains-dry our dark souls
Hollow hearts are time's fools
Buried gems never spoil
Deep beneath death's dank soil

Time slips beyond our grasp
Time waits and slyly laughs
Time fills the hourglass
Time fills the hourglass

Wake from the black abyss
Raised by your lover's kiss
Rise my jewel of the dead
All words we say, we've said

Remember love, we'll be
When futures we don't see
At some cold, distant place
Like our pasts, come too late

Time fills our hourglass
Time waits beyond our grasp
Time slips into our past
Time slips into our past

Psychedelic Lies

Dead-end memory of my mind
Your world revolves around your lies
Leave silhouette dreams behind
Cross painless, psychedelic skies

White, bottled nightmares on a tray
Illusion overshadows light
Taste the medicated day
Color the psychedelic night

Sleep endless, psychedelic lies
Drink purple, psychedelic dyes
Live under cold, white cotton sheets
Dream deep the psychedelic night

Boneyard buried in self-decay
Demented visions of our past
Sleep and call my tired name
Sweet, psychedelic dreams don't last

Sleep endless, psychedelic lies
Drink purple, psychedelic dyes
Live under cold, white cotton sheets
Dream deep the psychedelic night

LAURA'S LAIR

Wicked Laura's lair, bathed in perfumed smoke
Wiccan candle air, covers like a cloak
Wicked Laura's lair, drunk with demon blood
Dream the dark nightmare, black miasmal mud

Wicked Laura's lair, layered in worldly waste
Serpent of despair, tempts all boys to taste
Vile of the abyss, silver for a lie
Betrays with her kiss, whispers a goodbye

Hypnotized by Laura's stare
Ecstasy turns to despair
Euthanized in Laura's lair
Euthanized in Laura's lair

Wicked Laura's lair, breathe the gentle smoke
Tangled in her hair, wrapped around your throat
Wicked Laura's lair, death in satin sheets
Angel of despair, Satan never sleeps

Hypnotized by Laura's stare
Ecstasy turns to despair
Euthanized in Laura's lair
Wicked Laura's lair

Devil's night, hell's host

Zombie kindled in Poe's soul

Draven's ghost, crow's flight

Death's haunting shadow

Darts about pine coffin walls:

Darkest solitude

The Mōg

(a campfire tale)

Wind and lightning, beetle-brown pines
Whistle tales in the monsoon winds
Banshee stories, blazing bonfires
Whisper through crackling limbs

Ragtag troops of trembling Scouts
Curse rain from hell's thunder clouds
Cougar screams in the distance
Foreshadows death's dark shroud

The Mōg creeps up from the valley
Hidden deep on the Mōgollon Rim
Cold silver fangs and bloody claws
Tear through the forest timbs

The Mōg creeps up from the valley
Black and wet in the ghost-moon light
A monster born of mountain mire
Devours all by night

Bile burns in its fiery belly
Saliva drools down its grizzly chin
Mud mangled in matted beast hair
Filth spews from deep within

Scared Scouters run for cover
Ghoulish creature shreds their camp
Bodies carved, torn, broken
Khaki tents left crimson damp

The Mōg creeps up from the valley
Hidden deep on the Mōgollon Rim
Cold silver fangs and bloody claws
Tear through the forest timbs

The Mōg creeps up from the valley
Black and wet in the ghost-moon light
A monster born of mountain mire
Devours all by night

101

LA TIRANA

(The Legend of Huillac Ñusta)

Red snake wound around her hips
Death beneath her fingertips
Mesmerized by her demon spell
Feel her power, kiss her lips

Midnight hair and emerald eyes
Every word she speaks, a lie
Winter-white body cast in hell
A mystery never dies

She's a mystery, La Tirana
She's a mystery, La Tirana

Poison pleasure, heart of ice
Rocks your world, you roll the dice
Life is short when you buy and sell
Drink her wine, you pay the price

Spirits wrapped around our minds
Ghostly specters bleed us blind
Sinful souls never live to tell
Their dark secrets left behind

She's a mystery, La Tirana
She's a mystery, La Tirana

Baja Black

Buried in black
Covered in tar
Remnants of a perished star

Swimming in coal
Screeching, pitched bell
Hideous sound
No shirk from hell

Dripping in ink
A vagabond, cursed
Forever will sink
No quenching his thirst

Buried in black
Concealed in carbon
Forever to anguish
Never to pardon

By J. T. W.

ᴀPPARITION 31

As autumn permeates the dew,
Its cool briskness tingling, teasing
Summer's lively colors fade away
Sweet, subtle blush of falling leaves
Ghostly, revelatory glimpses
Rustling about the soggy earth,
Trapped in miniature whirlwinds,
Swirling crimson, gold, and amber,
Spices in a witch's cauldron
What frothy brew!
It steeps; they sleep,
Anticipating terror's warm taste
So tantalizingly near—

Pumpkins await the children's grasp
Vines harvest-dried, tangled
Each with twisted, singular form
Their caricature silhouettes lurking
Beneath fresh yellow-orange skins

Hidden from cruel, witching glare
Whispers of a midnight spell
Shadows thrown from faceless moon
Elongated, gruesome, contorted
Reaching across the dead ground
Eerie sounds reverberate darkest night
Ghouls, goblins, clowns, and familiar black cats
Creep into the chilly fog, then—

The dry language of the leaves murmurs,
"Hush, hush now
All Hallows' Eve is here."

By Andréa Watson

Ghosts of my journal—

Lost thoughts haunting forgotten

Pages: cursive souls

LA SIRENA

La Sirena sweeps across the coast
Whispers to her love
Warm winds through moonlit palms
Echo on the cove

She gathers in the village pub
A guitar softly strums
She drinks to nights of summer love
And sweet Bahaman rum

La Sirena sweeps across the coast
Phantasma of wind and light
La Sirena sweeps across the coast
A love song in the night

She runs her fingers through his hair
His heart beats with the waves
She wraps her lips around his mouth
Her siren soul, he craves

She takes his hand and leads him out
Beyond the coral sands
They disappear into the mist
Lovers without end

La Sirena sweeps across the coast
Phantasma of wind and light
La Sirena sweeps across the coast
A love song in the night

The ancient covenant path is narrow, painfully
difficult, and too seldom hiked; after all, there
are always two ways. That said, I'd rather be
at the bottom of the path, ascending, than at
the top, descending.

He shapes my desires;

Thus refined by holy fire,

My light burns brighter

Towers of crisp vines

Delineate sacred shapes

Around muddy pools

HOLY OF HOLIES, MOUNTAIN FIRE

Holy of Holies, Mountain Fire
    Save me from myself
Burn within me, true desire
    Purify my well
Holy of Holies, Great I Am
    Make my vision clear
The adversary clouds my mind
    Melt away my fear

Holy of Holies, thou art here
    Grant me peace today
True sanctuary of my soul
    Drive all doubt away
Holy of Holies, bread, and wine
    Bless my sacraments
Forgive me Lord and make me thine
    As I humbly now repent

Holy of Holies, Mountain Fire
    Heal me in my youth
Burn bright within me, Holiness
    Cleanse me by thy truth
Holy of Holies, Great I Am
    Dark clouds yet appear
Lord, help me ever to do thy will
    And feel thy firelight near

Holy of Holies, Mountain Fire
    Taste redeeming love
Holy of Holies, Mountain Fire
    Sealed by the Dove
Holy of Holies, Mountain Fire
    Feel our Master's love
Holy of Holies, Mountain Fire
    Know our God above

Watchers descend from

Celestial spheres: God's angels

Sent forth to protect

Late candlelight quests,

Searching wet cobblestone streets—

Lonely pathways home

The Olive Press

Brook of Cedron cleanses verdant skins
As winter waters wash across millstones
Blood of Christ, sacrificed for sin
Oh, Messiah, Lord, then flesh and bones
Olive press divides green fruit from oil
Where our Savior sweat great drops of blood
Air and sunlight time-taint and sometimes spoil
But we, saved by Eternal grace, His love

In that hallowed yard men press the paste
Beneath smooth discs of hemp and granite
Gethsemane, sacred crushing place
Where only the purest oil's decanted
In the garden Christ atoned for every soul
By midnight moon He crushed the serpent's hate
And with the fate of all in holy hands
His sacrifice unlocked the heavenly gate

Brook of Cedron cleanses verdant skins
As winter waters wash across millstones
Blood of Christ sanctifies from sin
Oh, Messiah, Lord, then flesh and bones
Dear Father, wilt thou remove this bitter cup
Of guilt and pain and earthly sorrow
If not, I now gladly drink it up
And hang on wooden cross tomorrow

We're baptized for our worldly sins
Like fresh olives washed in water
He renews the souls of women and men
Through His precious blood, His light, His honor
Glory be to the Master, King of Kings
Anointed by our dear Eternal Father
Praise His name in temples, Earth, and Heaven
Every angel, saint, sweet son, and daughter

God does weep; "But why?"

We ask, witnessing holy

Temple's destruction

Stand, brave bison king!

Fight fiercely, Great Plains warrior!

Rise with the white Sun.

Adorned, true garments

of light, Christ Jesus transcends;

Mystery revealed

OMPHALÓS

Celestial spirits
Descend through space, quickening
Physical bodies;
Omphalós—
Life's fragile mortals
Pass through time's ports, harboring
Spiritual souls.

Sky kings, seraphim,

Andean bearers of light—

Drink nectars' knowledge

Helaman's striplings,

Forge-welded, layered, polished,

Sheathed in God's armor

THE NAZCA
LINES

From River Sidon
They walked the Bountiful line
To the west seashore

A day and a half's
Journey between Bountiful
And Desolation

A pathway across
Nazca's narrow neck of land?
A border of shells?

Who laid the measures?
Who stretched the lines upon it?
Ghost signs in the sand

LIAHONA:
LIGHT OF PARACAS?

"To God is the Guidance"

I watched an Incan fisherman
Sketch wisdom in the low tide sand
Like the geoglyphs at Nazca
Mysteries drawn by ancient hands

I pondered the Candelabra's
Glow on the mountainside at dusk
Did dry winds of the Sechura
Whisper scripture out of thy dust?

Humble people of Paracas
Wandering barks beneath the stars
Liahona, shining compass
Brass reflection of faithful hearts

I dreamed of civilizations
Where petrified sands fell like rain
And conquerors rode waves of lust
Tempest tossed from the shores of Spain

Prayerful people of Paracas
Forever know God's guiding ways
Was Liahona, true compass,
Carved in rock over Pisco Bay?

(Written while contemplating "El Candelabro" geoglyph of
Pisco Bay, Peru and the design, structure, and engineering
of an early nineteenth-century spinning wheel—its base,
supports, bobbin, maidens, and "spindles.")

Shine forth upon me,

Constellation of God's love:

Wondrous Tree of Life

My love, what remains

At day's end, starry nightfall,

Is eternal peace

"Poet, lift up your head and follow me,"

whispers a still, small voice.

ABOUT
THE AUTHOR

S. C. Watson is a prize-winning poet and writer residing in Show Low, Arizona, nestled high in the ponderosa forests of the White Mountains. He holds a BA degree in English from Brigham Young University and a JD degree from Willamette University College of Law. He is co-owner of Baja Bad Press, a small, family-run publishing company, and the author of *Baja Bad*, a collection of original gothic, religious, and Southwestern prose, and lyric poetry.

He has traveled throughout Mexico, South America, and Spain and speaks fluent Spanish. He attributes his creative writing training to his studies under renowned Welsh poet Leslie Norris and American writer Bruce W. Jorgensen. He is also an active member of the Arizona State Poetry Society.

He is married to talented artist and photographer Andréa, who illustrates their books. They can be reached at BajaBadPress@gmail.com.